Dream Castles

.

Dream Castles

Antonia B. Laird

To Andrea and Hugh
and Blake

with best wishes.
Toni Laird

Rutledge Books, Inc.   **RB**   Danbury, CT

Rutledge Books, Inc.
107 Mill Plain Road, Danbury, CT 06811
1-800-278-8533
www.rutledgebooks.com

Manufactured in the United States of America

Cataloging in Publication Data
Laird, Antonia B.
    Dream Castles

    ISBN: 1-58244-199-5

    1. Poetry

Library of Congress Control Number: 2001098661

Dedicated to
my family with love

Contents

DREAM CASTLES

At night
I build dream castles
in the air.
How grand they seem
when all the room
is dark with just a sliver
of the moon
beneath the shade.
I write the mystery
novel of the year,
Compose a waltz,
walk down a private beach
on pure white sand.
Forever young,
I dance with Fred Astaire,
hear violins
in mirrored ballrooms
high above the sea.
As dawn awakes,
my castles crumble
to the ground
and all their turrets disappear.

Full moon,
how can one so far away
control our night
and send us sleepless
toward another day.
So powerful your rays
you reach
behind the window shades,
and send me tossing
in a restless sea of sheets.
You are to blame
for aches and pains,
until you turn your face away
and hide your witchcraft
from the breath of day.

WILL WE MEET

Will we meet
when winter
wears an ermine coat,
or will the leaves
be dressed in green
when first you smile?
Seasons pass,
summer into fall,
and still I look
behind each face,
to find you waiting
in a warm enchanted place.

FIREWORKS

Fireworks explode
across the sky,
thin rockets shooting
from the ground
to burst
above the trees
into a thousand colored
points of light.
A half-moon flirts
between the clouds
to watch the fountains'
water dance.
While music plays
majestic notes,
cascades of diamonds
fill the air
with beauty on a Longwood night.

Longwood Garden, Pennsylvania

Is it the sport of kings,
or only jesters
at the court who play?
It's hard to tell.
For everyone
it seems a hell
one day,
a paradise the next,
a nightmare game
one plays against oneself.
I move too quickly
for this boring sport,
I have no patience
for a practice swing,
I'd rather fling
the club after the ball.
But still I play.
They say
that golf's addictive
and I find,
that I have lost forever
peace of mind.

THE GOLF FOURSOME

Golf teaches patience,
waiting is the essence of the game.
Each partner's practice swing
becomes the rhythm of your mind
as well as theirs.
So many minutes pass
before your turn
that every lesson learned
is lost before you swing.
Four hours later we are through;
why don't we play again
just me and you?

GREAT HORNED OWL

Great owl
how wise you are
to hide at night
among the trees,
so handsome with your
fine white throat
and yellow eyes.
No rodent traveling
through your woods is safe,
for while the world's asleep
your talons carry off
your evening meal.
Nocturnal cat,
beware this creature
with a head
that swivels left and right,
and stay indoors
and warm my feet instead.

SUDDEN DEATH

Is it fate or luck
that plays the final hand,
that chooses who will
live another day,
or who will die
before the secondhand
has swept across the clock?
One morning
you were there
and now you're gone.
Was there a spirit
high above
who plucked your number
from a crowded line,
or did a bell in heaven
start to ring,and all the angels
sing—"It's time!"

THE AMERICAN CEMETERY

In perfect rows they march
across a battlefield of green,
in straight formations
that will never move again.
Christians and Jews, a cross, a star,
they lie together as they fought
across the German's strong defense
to set France free.
A marble statue stands,
a young man coming from the sea . . .
he looks across the vast unending rows
of those who rest in peace,
forever young,
while those they love grow old.

Normandy

How beautiful the flowers are
in front of every tall white cross
that marks a grave.
So many fine young Englishmen
laid down their lives forever
in this foreign land.
Each cross engraved,
a saying from the heart
of those who mourn.
A boy, a man, who never
would come home
to smell the flowers
of an English spring.

Normandy

THE GERMAN CEMETARY

Here rest the German dead,
beneath dark stone they lie
entombed forever,
never knowing that their war
to rule the world was lost.
Left to mark their sad young lives
are grave sites
in a land they learned to hate
and fought to conquer
on a summer day.

Normandy

LAST YEAR

A sadness fills my heart
between the memories
and the tears,
steals the sunlight
from a summer day.
The view of lake and mountains
are the same
we saw last year,
but now I watch alone
a rainbow in an Adirondack Sky
and wish that death had passed you by.

A WALLED GARDEN

A walled garden,
silence only broken
by the sound of birds
calling out their news.
Azaleas bloom,
bouquets of color
in their pine brown beds.
A gray cat stalks
on silk-soft paws,
traps a lizard,
biting off its head.

CAMELIA PINK PARADE

Her petals hide no fragrance
in their soft embrace,
they hold no competition
with a rose,
no thorns,
but only pointed leaves
and slender stems
enhance her soft pink face,
a blush of beauty
by a southern wall.

CHIONANTHUS VIRGINICUS

The fringe tree's blossoms
hang like small white beards
on branches stretched
across the terrace wall.
Their fragrance floats
across the air
like perfume from a petal flask
that nature purchased
on a warm spring day.

HOPEFUL EXPECTATIONS

Anticipation wears an eager face
waiting for the moment with a smile,
hoping expectations will be met,
an evening that you never will forget.

The music plays, he's asked you for a dance
beneath a sky that's luminous with light,
a twinkle in his eye, a soft caress,
no need to ask the answer will be yes.

FUR FRIENDS

Why do some people hate all cats
and quiver when they scamper by,
perhaps their parents told them lies
when they were young?
Cats won't steal the breath away
of babies lying in their beds,
or ride with witches on a broom,
or sit on gravestones by the dead.
They're loving friends well dressed in fur
who lie beside your feet at night
and greet you with a soft meow,
if you are kind and treat them right.

Majestic one,
don't flap your ears
and wave your trunk
at me.
Your size impresses
everyone
without the pounding
of your wrinkled feet,
the bellow of your lungs.
I'm scared you'll charge,
but if it's just a nuisance tease
go back to eating
summer leaves,
and I'll retrieve
my heart
that skipped a beat!

A SUMMER RAINBOW

We'd gather on the boathouse porch
to shelter from the heavy rain,
and found ourselves with front row seats
to watch a rainbow fill the sky.
An island caught its colored tail
and tossed it to the distant shore,
it pierced the ruffles of the lake
before a fading last goodbye.
We found no fabled pot of gold
that afternoon in Saranac,
but never will our hearts forget
that rainbow in our summer sky.

A WET ADIRONDACK SUMMER

The forecast is for rain again
more tears from heaven
running down the leaves.
The grass is drenched, jewel green,
every footprint shows.
The moss has never looked so lush.
The sun is waiting
for an autumn day to shine.
With all the tourists gone
he'll show his face,
all warm and smooth
without a trace of tears.

ONE LOON ALONE

One loon
for days has been alone
as though he's anchored
off our shore,
he rides the waves
his feathers ruffled by the wind.
He hardly moves
except to fish.
His call a haunting melody
of other summers
when he had a friend.

BLACK CAT ON THE FLOAT

Black cat
how still you sit,
so regal on the float,
serene.
The waterskiers pass you by
and not a whisker twitches,
not a protest or a purr.
You scare the seagulls
but you don't fool me.
My cat with soft, gray fur
would never stand
for waves beneath
and not an honest mouse in sight.

STEPPING STONES

Last night's rain
has turned the moss
into a chain
of islands
in a wet, brown sea.
Green velvet mounds
that hug the earth,
make stepping stones
for bare feet
on a summer day.

TREE SKIING

We weave
a ribbon through the trees
on snow
that hasn't felt a skier's track,
around the aspens'
slender trunks
we go, ski dancing
on a powder floor
where snowshoe rabbits
left their prints
the night before.

TALL VERSUS SHORT

We are the handsomest of all,
the tall trees said,
our heads are closer
to the sky
while you can only shiver
in the shadow of our height.
The small trees
smiled and waited for
the first snowflakes to fall
and dress them in a thick
white plume of white,
for with the snow
came winter's cold, cruel breath
that stripped the tall trees
of their winter hats
and left them bald.

A STORM OF WORDS

After the rain
the trees still weep
their gentle tears
as I do
once the hurricane
of words have passed
and I am left alone.
Another storm will come
but I'll not wait
for thunder and the chance
of rain
when there is sunlight
on a different shore.

The Social Register
has come
and you're not in it,
what a shame!
Perhaps your name
has been misspelled
or just misplaced
in someone's office
full of names
that fill the social pages
of the news.
You haven't been divorced
or made a scene,
I'm sure they'd let you know
if this were so.
Maybe you're of southern birth,
with a pedigree supreme,
and do not want a book
to share you're name.

PLASTIC SURGERY

The surgeon with his practical eyes
and hands so skilled they capture youth,
can sew away the finest lines
and hide the truth.
Like snow that covers every trace
of how the garden looked before,
the vanished lines have left behind
an empty face.

SOLITAIRE

A game for one
to fill empty hours
of the day.
No skill involved, just one card on another,
black to red.
How sad when life is Solitaire
instead of Hearts.

DEPRESSION

Surrounded by a wall of fog
that wind or rain can't blow away
that settles into every cell
until life is turned to hell.
A mind that's wrapped in cotton wool
that medicines can't seem to tear
psychiatrists have talked their fill
but nothing helps, it's all downhill.
Much easier to mend a leg
or cut a poisoned tumor out,
then cure a mind that's gone astray
how sad, we miss you every day.

ONE LONE CHAIR

One lone chair
beside the pond,
the one who put it there
has gone
to fly beyond a distant place,
where even make-believe
is real,
and two chairs wait beside a pond
to hear the angels sing.

ELUSIVE PAIN

The master of the game of hide and seek,
elusive fellow with sharp nails of steel,
you climb into a crevice of the brain,
your fingers stretch in octaves head to heel.
An avalanche that swirls across the eyes,
swoops down with force that seems to have no end,
then disappears as though a wizard's wand
had turned the enemy into a friend.

A WET MORNING

Wet paws
and matted fur
are not what
one gray cat
expects when he
wakes up and cries
to taste the pleasures
of a garden stroll.
Don't turn your back
and stalk away from me
fur friend,
I'm not in charge
of what the heavens send
to spoil your day,
I'll stroke behind
your ears and make
your anger fade away.

"Haste makes waste"
or so the old wives said,
but how were they to know
that slow is not a word
I understand.
My brain is set
on just one speed,
my feet obey
and through the day
refuse to change.
But when the moon
ascends her lofty throne
and all small children
hate to go to bed,
I race to cover up
my restless feet,
and let my eyes
dart down the printed page.

CATARACT SURGERY

New eyes have swept the years away,
the mist is gone, it's bright as day,
but friends now suddenly look old,
each wrinkle stands out clear and bold.
When doctors work on old men's eyes
and makes them young as well as wise,
remember age is in the mind,
the face thinks young although it's lined.

TV

My square black box
has tentacles
that reach across the room,
wrap themselves
around my brain
to draw me in.
The history channel
or a game of golf
becomes my ticket
to this television world,
where British sitcoms
are a tame addiction
in a square black box.

ENVY

Envy came to battle
with a polished shield,
a sharp thin blade of steel
to pierce the heart,
and in her head
the beating of a jealous drum.
Fall back, I cry
no battle in this room today,
I will not fight
a monster
with a false green smile.

I'm tethered by so many strings
I cannot fly,
although I've never wanted
to before.
The sky is much too far away,
and clouds are sometimes dark
and full of rain.
One summer day
I might use scissors
when the air is hung
with honeysuckle vines,
the sky deep blue
as far as I can see,
but I'll return
before the barn owl calls my name,
I've never wanted to fly free.

TO MY PARENTS AND GRANDPARENTS

I live surrounded
by the history of another age,
when pride was built into a chair
and porcelain shaped itself
into a teapot or a bowl.
I sit upon a Queen Anne chair,
eat dinner from a Chinese plate
and wonder who has dined
with them before.
Possessions own me
not the other way around,
I hold on loan
the beauty of two hundred years
and all the treasured memories
of collectors
I held dear.

MINIATURE TEA SETS

There was a world of let's pretend
two hundred years ago or more,
where young girls practiced serving tea
from pots no larger than a key.
Miniatures of fine creamware
or porcelain in the latest style,
were not just used for girlish play
but bought by ladies to display.
High on an antique dealer's shelf,
away from children's tiny hands,
there waits a tea set, blue and white,
born in the years of candlelight.

Anchored by your chains
you can't swim far
my two white swans.
I know you're made of wood
and can't escape,
but when at dusk
the water ripples by your wings,
I almost feel you'll
slip your chains
and fly away.

OMAGH

The bus turned quickly
but we still could see
bouquets of flowers
placed against a wall,
a view of windows
dressed in wood
instead of glass,
an empty space
to show what bombs can do
without a thought to age
or race,
or loved ones
lost forever on an August day.
This passing scene
has left a memory
that will last
beside the beauty of great gardens,
houses, people that we met
in two short weeks.
What sadness in a land
where sheep graze peacefully
in fields of green.

Northern Ireland

BEING ALONE

Being alone
is not being lonely,
It's a long walk
on a wide beach
where the only sound
is a bird's cry,
the wind racing a blue sky
and surf riding the shore.
Loneliness
is being alone
with a room full of people
who don't care,
when despair is a tear
on a frozen check
in a bright room

A slower pace allows
the time to smile,
while speaking
with a softer voice
that wraps the words
in honey and a Southern drawl.
The colder climates
sound a stronger tone
no time to smile-
when worlds rush quickly
from a freezing throat.

MORNING FOG AT OCEAN FOREST

The golf course
closed in fog
wore mystery
like a large concealing cloak,
outlines
of trees
along a fairway
hardly seen.
Birds were silent,
still asleep,
or mesmerized
by drifts of gray.
We played
while cold, damp fingers
stroked our hair,
and hit our ball
we knew not where.

Sea Island, Georgia

Small eaglet
were you born
afraid to fly
while both your parents
soar above you
in an early April sky?
You've left the safety
of your nest and perch
upon a branch,
come, take a chance
and test your wings
on air.
Day after day we see
your undecided stance,
until one morning,
high above our heads,
you say good-bye,
and ride the rhythm
of a conquered sky.

OSPREYS

Two ospreys built a sturdy nest
high in the tallest red pine tree,
they fly above the golfers' heads
then circle quickly down to fish.
Their dinner grasped in greedy claws
they sail above in graceful flight,
while golfers pitch and putt below,
young ospreys seize a tasty dish.

LIVE OAK TREES

Live oaks arch above the road,
one branch stetching to another.
Dressed in tangled Spanish moss
they spread their beauty as they reach across.

Small leaves flutter to the ground,
one season turning to another.
Each generation sings their praise,
a Southern beauty from a golden age.

A CHEERLESS SKY

A cheerless sky,
dark clouds that skim
above the trees,
turn the faces
of the waves to gray.
A gloomy barricade
that threatens rain,
until one shaft of light
breaks through the clouds
with just a subtle promise
of a brighter day.

Gentle giant
with a noble head,
soft brown eyes
that beg to jump
upon my bed
and settle down.
A coat that waves
and curls beneath
my hand,
a large white paw
across my arm,
and so we nap,
two friends
who share an afternoon.

All light is gone
and there is only night
that stretches down a lonely path
toward dawn.
Minutes drag by step by step
for sleep has fled,
and taken all his dreams
to peaceful beds
where there are smooth, clean sheets
and soft white pillows
stuffed with down.
"Come back," I cry,
"and hold me in your arms,
close down my eyelids
with a kiss,
and let me lie beside you
until dawn."

CHAMPAGNE

Champagne,
moonlight,
a terrace
close beside the sea.
Champagne,
music,
strong arms
encircling you to me.
Champagne
bubbling,
roses
in a crystal vase.
Champagne,
dancing,
waltz my love
through nights and days.

AFTER TEN P.M.

You have a salad
of a mind,
each word is tossed
with thought
and splashed
with wit.
At dinner you are
at your best,
against your repartee
gray politicians lose their voice
"Young Turks" know less,
you are the sparkle
and the glow.
But after ten
your brilliance fades
and goes to bed,
your words sit listless
in an even row.

A FULL MOON THIEF

The room is dark,
the blackout shades
have made a nighttime cave
where I lie sleepless
in a tangled web.
I toss and turn
and wait for morning
and its loud alarm.
Although quite hidden
by the clouds and rain
the full moon plays
its monthly game,
I am captive
in my earthbound bed.